TO SING
HALLUCINATED

First Thoughts
on Last Words

MEZCALITA PRESS, LLC
Norman, Oklahoma

MEZCALITA PRESS, LLC
Norman, Oklahoma

Also by Nathan Brown:

Less Is More, More or Less
Karma Crisis: New and Selected Poems
Letters to the One-Armed Poet
My Sideways Heart
Two Tables Over
Not Exactly Job
Suffer the Little Voices
Ashes Over the Southwest
Hobson's Choice

Edited by Nathan Brown:

Oklahoma Poems, and Their Poets

Edited by Ashley and Nathan Brown:

Agave: A Celebration of Tequila in Story, Song, Poetry,
Essay, and Graphic Art

They are strange but simple folk who sing
hallucinated by a brilliant point of light
trembling on the horizon.

~ Federico García Lorca

TO SING
HALLUCINATED

First Thoughts
on Last Words

~ Nathan Brown ~

TABLE OF CONTENTS

Acknowledgements

Thanks to Kellie Salome for gifting me the book that inspired this one.

Thanks to Ronald E. Moore, Dan Williams, George Wallace, and Michael & Joyce Gullickson for publishing some of these poems first.

Unlike Father, Unlike Son; Venom; As a Dying Man Always Does; Nevertheless, It Moves appeared in the anthology *8 Voices: Contemporary Poetry from the American Southwest* (Baskerville Publishers, 2012).

Going Ahead appeared in the online magazine *Poetrybay.* Fall/Winter 2014 issue.

A Question of Prefixes appeared in *Blue Hole 2015.*

And What For? appeared in *The Enigmatist 2015.*

Thanks to Ashley Brown, the best poetry editor I know (even though she's the only), Chris Everett, Rodney Bursiel, R.C. Davis, Terri Stubblefield, George Economou, and Corky and Vicki Melass.

A special thanks to my parents, Lavonn and Norma Brown, for having made pretty much everything possible over the last fifty years.

To Sierra, my daughter, you are always...

As ever... and ever will be... Ashley.

In honor and memory of

~ E. A. "Tony" Mares ~

a good soul and poet...
a friend and fellow traveler...

~ 1938 – 2015 ~

TO SING
HALLUCINATED

First Thoughts
on Last Words

Crito, we owe a cock to Asclepius.
Do pay it. Don't forget.

~ Socrates, 399 BC

MY QUESTIONS

Doesn't it seem like Socrates
should have asked a question
as the hemlock made its way up
from toes to knees to the heart?
Isn't that what we'd loved him for?

Could it be that his whole thing—
the questioning everything thing—
had been a philosophical gimmick,
just some sad professional shtick,
he grew tired of towards the end?

Or could it have been that after all
the fun and questions, he finally
had to face the truest of truths,
that right up to the day we die
we've got to pay the bills?

Everything will shortly be turned upside down.

~ Diogenes the Cynic, 323 BC

PLEASE. NO MORE.

Yesterday, in Oklahoma,
we had a generous number
of gully-washers that flooded
and choked the drought-dead
plains and bloodshot creek beds.

Gully-washers that brought along
sheets of hail and several tornados
that sliced and whipped their way
through a string of cityless counties
in what would seem like nowhere
to someone from Massachusetts.

Tornados that spun their rage,
tearing through red-brick houses
and ravaging cinderblock buildings
as if they had teeth made of diamonds.

Diamonds the evening had just put away
when a 4.7 magnitude earthquake rocked
and then rolled parts of this mostly
decent, gritty, and resilient state.

The earthquake being the only goody
in nature's gift bag our state doesn't
expect. One we would like to return
to the big store in Los Angeles.

My God, my God, why hast thou forsaken me?

~ Jesus of Nazareth

UNLIKE FATHER, UNLIKE SON

There were those days
he didn't want the job.

Remember the hard cup
in the garden, that stuff
he didn't want to drink?
But his dad made him
take of it anyway?

Must be tough to live
with a father like that.

You've come to save the world
and everywhere you go—
restaurants, theaters, bars—
everyone wants to talk to Him.

Maybe that's why his mother
cried at the foot of the cross.

She knew how long it would take
for people to realize her son
was the better man.

THE PAPER BURNS,
BUT THE WORDS FLY FREE

~ Akiba ben Joseph, 135

All this striving
   for permanence.
Carve. Print. Embalm.

Some 32,000 years ago
a teenager in south France
decides that he does not want
to join the hunting party today.

He will just stay at home, alone,
like any normal brooding artiste,
and paint the tragedy of spears
on the walls of his cave instead.

And 32,000 years later we marvel
at his finished and faded product,
offering our overeducated guesses
as to his intentions, and building
a national park for public viewing.

When, in truth, the kid simply had
some chemical imbalance he'd tried
to work out through an inexplicable
urge. And, most likely, his mother
had encouraged him to do it.

She was a woman of surpassing beauty.

~ Cassius Dio speaking of Cleopatra, c. 210 to 230

VENOM

No rest for the beautiful.
But especially for those
of surpassing beauty
and egregious wealth.

All of that royal drama,
wrestling Caesars for power.
Everyone in and out of their
togas all the time. A son here,
maybe a few others over there.

Her baths in fresh goat's milk...
    the silk of snake-like charms.
Antony's ill-fated battle at sea...
    and suicide over the loss.

Then, the snap of fangs,
the bites
        of two asps,
as tradition demands,
and they all fall down.

I have loved justice and hated iniquity;
therefore I die in exile.

~ Pope St. Gregory VII, 1085

GOES WITH THE JOB

Stick a holy hand
in the face of kings
and strip them of their
ecclesiastical privileges,

then go right to work on
reforming God himself
while outlawing sex
for his leading men,

and tell me, honestly,
that you were surprised
by your harsh deposition
at the Synod of Worms.

Or the eventual siege
of Rome. Or that you
might fall far enough
to have to be rescued

by some greasy Norman
named Robert the Weasel,
before they caught you again
and whisked you quietly away.

We are continually dying; I while I am writing these
words, you while you are reading them, others when they
hear them or fail to hear them.

~ Petrarch
Letter to a Friend, c. 1360, died 1374

GO EASY

Well, isn't this just the biggest
glass o' half empty ever served?

Petrarch was a poet, however.
And we do have such a hard time
keeping our feet on the bridge rail,
and then our heads above the filth
once we're in the current below.

To his credit though, he survived
the worst the plague had to offer
while losing everyone to it—
    including that special one
    who spawned two decades
    of unrequited sonnets.

And we cannot ignore his part
in birthing the term *Dark Ages*—
a name to help his generation
realize how much counseling
and therapy their children
would soon be needing.

All told, it's hard to believe
he made it to one day shy

of his 70th birthday.

One day shy. One last
little cautionary sign.

Lest we pour
a bit too much
in our glasses.

Hold the cross high so I may see it
through the flames!

~ Joan of Arc, 1431

AND WHAT FOR?

So many burned at the stake.
For God. For not believing.
For believing too much.
Or believing in something
besides what they were told
to believe by the church.

It took little in the way
of theological detours
to spark the suspicion
of bishops and priests,
or to fuel their fixation
with wood and flames.

And Joan. Poor Joan.
The Maid of Orleans.
Another poet betrayed
by the little voices—
voices sent by God.

So why *wouldn't* she tell
the ecclesiastical court?

And in her defense, anyone
who has ever heard them,
knows what she means.

As a Dying Man Always Does…

~ Lorenzo the Magnificent, 1492

… ask for one last margarita,
    with salt and a lime wedge,
      and for the window
      to be opened wide.

… tell the king to go to hell,
    and to your sister say…
      you never much cared for
      her husband or the middle son.

… have someone light a candle,
    maybe fluff the pillows…
      please, one more time.

… demand a shot of tequila, straight,
    to wash down the margarita,
      as you rip all those needles
      and tubes out of your veins.

… go silent…
    for a time…
      and hope your loved ones
      don't want you to go. Not yet.

… and then, for God's sake,
    think of one
    last thing
    to say.

WAIT A MINUTE
~ Pope Alexander VI, 1503

Maybe he'd wanted
to explain something.
Or maybe to apologize
for that party he threw
in the apostolic palace—

    the one where he'd had
    the naked exotic dancers
    lap chestnuts off the floor
    before he took his pick.

We've deserved as much
from a good number
of religious leaders
over the millennia.

    And this last century,
    with its Charlie Mansons
    and Southern Baptists,
    was not an exception.

Anyway, I imagine God
allows them ample time
to clarify a few things
when they get over
to the other side.

Pluck up thy spirits, man, and be not afraid to do thine office, my neck is very short. Take heed therefore thou shoot not awry...

~ Sir Thomas More, 1535

I heard say the executioner was very good, and I have a little neck.

~ Anne Boleyn, 1536

WHAT WE GET

We prefer a smaller gathering
of the better family at the end.
Maybe a best friend or two.
Maybe some last little tickle
from warm fingers of love.

And we have a few things
we want to say to them.

But sometimes,
we speak only lost words
right before the loud shatter
of headlights and windshields,
or the sudden loss of our grip
on the cliff's crumbling edge.

Other times, our company—
final counselor and confidant—
wears the dark woolen hood
and holds the big axe.

14

IT CAME WITH A LASS,
IT WILL PASS WITH A LASS

~ James V, King of Scotland, 1542

Though I don't know
exactly what you meant,
I feel it in my marrow
and know what I mean.

It comes with them...
    it passes with them,
the women in our lives.

And I know the second line
was for your six-day-old Mary,
Queen of Scots—your lost
last hope for one male heir.

Those daughters can be such
a fine and blesséd torture, all
the way to their untimely ends.

So, in your own final days,
when melancholy grew teeth
and quaked inside your skull,
I'm just sorry the good doctors
had no Prozac or Zoloft for you
in their black Gladstone bags.

Monks! Monks! Monks!

~ King Henry VIII, 1547

KINGS! QUEENS! CONSORTS!

One fat man with a crown,
and a short string of six wives,
did not a happy England make.

    All of Rome's cathedrals,
    its monasteries and abbeys,
    burning bright in their wake.

And four of those queens
died before him in a havoc
of deceit and covered tracks.

    One in an exile of sadness.
    One from the fever. Two
    by the sharpened axe.

And so, after turning
all the nuns into beggars,
and all of the monks into bums,

    they haunted his royal hallucinations
    when he finally heard the beating
    of his own death's drums.

I have nothing, owe a great deal, and the rest I leave to
the poor.

~ François Rabelais, 1553

GOOD FOR NOTHIN'

A friar and a monk.
Yet every novel he wrote
made the Vatican's voluminous
"Index of Forbidden Books."

Far too much honesty
about sex and bungholes.
    Too much open love for wine
    and filling the vacuums of life.
        Too many jokes and jabs
        at the Holy Church.

The preacher's kid in me—
    what little is left of him—
paid dearly for all the above. But
not as dearly as the good Rabelais.

These days, if the Baptists boycott
a book, it only increases its sales.

Still, after all accounts are settled,
the will and testament carried out,
I'll have nothing, owe a great deal,
and leave the same amount
of naught to the poor.

Now I'm oiled.
Keep me from the rats.

~ Pietro Aretino, 1556

RAMPAGE

It is exhilarating to find your own
16th Century Italian doppelganger,
my Renaissance partner in crime,
a poet who goes that far back
beyond the great Bukowski—

someone some dry historian
bothered to coin "the father
of pornographic writing," one
who terrorized Dukes, princes,
even their precious princesses,
taking pot-shots at politicians
and the Pope's pet elephant.

Imagine mere sonnets
inciting a holy order
for his assassination.

No one was safe.
No one could stop him.

Until he finally…
laughed himself to death.

You will not find me alive at sunrise.

~ Nostradamus, 1566

TO KNOW… OR NOT TO KNOW…

How much do we want to know about
what dreams and death may come?

Did Nostradamus foresee London
burning like a stack of dry kindling
a hundred years after his death?
Or, was it merely a poetic guess?
13,000 houses burned nonetheless.
And all those Londoners still died
in the smoke and sea of flames.

Growing up I never knew
how much I loved going to bed
not knowing what mom would cook
for breakfast on the following morning.
I didn't know what a joy it was not to have
the sense of triangulation that I have now,
like on the drive home after Thanksgiving,
knowing I-35 will limp and crawl along
like some great failed apocalypse—
    how that three-hundred-mile river
    of tail-lights and exhaust will look
    like the Book of Revelation burning
    on the horizon of the 21st Century…

and how I'll wish to be dead by sunrise.

NEVERTHELESS, IT MOVES

~ Galileo, 1642

You took away our center,
displaced us, moved us away from
the command post of God's universe,
    then you stuck some bright star,
    a burning ball with no soul,
    there in our place instead.

How did you think the cardinals
and bishops would react to the news,
    after they'd gone to all that trouble
    having their elaborate gowns tailored,
    not to mention the huge expense
    of those great and gaudy hats?

Maybe at sixty-nine you saw a certain
allure in the conditions of house arrest.
    I'm in my late forties, and I'll tell you,
    it's crossed my mind a time or two.

Maybe you saw more in that telescope
than you were prepared to tell us.

Either way, the more I mull over
    your defiant last words,
the more I want to say them out loud
    to everyone I meet.

More weight!

~ Giles Corey, 1692

A PRESSING SITUATION

That cold autumn
in the 17th Century
was truly a bad time
to be a decent farmer
suspected of witchcraft
by a few good young girls
eating some bad mushrooms
back in the thick and beautiful
woods of eastern Massachusetts.

And so it was that the pious folks
of Salem Village stuck yet another
fat and holy foot into the wide open
mouth of religion, showing once again
its deadly magnetism to the misguided.

That's why, though you married four times,
I speak with such a deep and gory admiration
of your unimaginable and mulish convictions.

To say nothing, make no wheezing confession,
as they stripped you, laid you down, and began
to stack those stones upon your bare chest.
And, in such a pressing situation, beg
for nothing, except more rocks.

Well! A woman that can fart is not yet dead!

~ La Contessa Thérèse di Vercellis, 1728

RED WINE AND RIBS

I've had the privilege,
and sometimes pleasure,
of keeping a judicious variety
of company over the years.
        Many good women.
            A fewer good men.

I've dined with prime ministers
in Jerusalem's great Knesset.

        I've sipped cheap red wine
        out of conical paper cups
        on the bare kitchen floor
        of a stripper's apartment.

I've sampled the olive medley
and swigged $50 margaritas
in Hemingway's hidden bar
around back at the Paris Ritz.

        And I've munched the spare
        meat of smoked deer ribs
        in the backyards of Texas.

So, here at the top of the 21st Century,
and at the base of my next 50 years,
I'd like to scrape this in the bark
of the Tree of Life:

If it does indeed
come down to the choice
between gold and greed,
   or love and all its art...

I'll ride on into my sunset
by the firepit and fellowship
of good bitches and bastards
who live to eat, drink, and fart.

And when it comes time to climb
that final old set of squeaky stairs,
may they die in my hard company,
and I...   in theirs.

Here am I, dying of a hundred good symptoms.

~ Alexander Pope, 1744

PHILOSOPHICAL THOUGHTS
OVER A GLASS OF GOOD TEQUILA

I have a little something new,
a pain that keeps bothering me,
somewhere down and to the back.

But I still have not had enough time
for the tests I need before the surgery
to deal with whatever has afflicted me
for two years up here and to the front.

And when I weigh the barium swallows,
scopes and probes—all those violations
to a man's body and waning dignity,
things much worse in some ways
than the maladies themselves—

it's enough to make me consider
yanking my investments, emptying
all accounts, and betting the lot of it
on the chilled glass and salted rim

of one good cure.

Après nous, le déluge.
After us, the deluge.

~ Madame de Pompadour, 1764

APRÈS MOI

After us, comes
the narcissistic flood,

    that massive wave
    we believe will crash
    on the future's shore,
    annihilating all art, culture,
    and every iota of good taste,
        if not humans as a species,
        when we're no longer around
        to save them from themselves.

And I have no idea what
Madame de Pompadour
meant when she said this
to the lecherous Louis XV,

    but I'm certain the world
    will continue to get better,
    or worse,
            after me.

> I only regret that I have but one life to lose
> for my country.
>
> ~ Nathan Hale, 1776

WRINKLES IN THE FLAG

I am not a good patriot.
   I would not care to die
      for this or any country.

I reserve that kind of rashness
for my sweet wife and daughter.
And even for their sakes I'd shake
and quiver in my socks and boots,
like a terrified child before the axe.

Yet if dying be the key qualification
for a patriot, I know not one elected
beast up high on that great white hill,

senator, representative, elephant or ass,
who would, after all that hot air and ash,
willingly step up to the dangling noose.

Though, they do send in their stead
every possible high school graduate
they can get their lined palms on.
   (Save their own, of course.)

That said, I'd love to see
any damn one of them
prove me wrong.

THIS IS NO TIME TO MAKE NEW ENEMIES

~ Voltaire, 1778

...though, it would be
the easiest time to do it
    ...the perfect time
    to get the last laugh...
    and finally not be joking.

And it is true, Voltaire was
cracking wise about Satan.

But I guess I never stopped
to consider what an incredible
opportunity it is to be afforded
a quick minute or two to say
one   last   thing.

And to have someone
present there to hear it.

                    I wonder,
do better minds
prepare and rehearse
their closing statements?

If so, I feel a sudden pressure.

The first step toward philosophy is incredulity.

~ Denis Diderot, 1784

A QUESTION OF PREFIXES

I incline towards disbelief.
As opposed to unbelief.
I have never felt a need
for there not to be a God.

I just worried, even as a kid,
that the pious all around me
were... well... uncredible.

As opposed to my dad, a pastor,
who is among the more credible
humans I have ever known—
I'd go as far as to say incredible.

It's just that I've enjoyed disbelieving.
Or, let's say, the sin of questioning—
a key weapon in the great battle
against unbelieving, I believe.

Possibly even a means
to someday rebelieving.

Throw a quilt over it.

~ Frederick the Great, Frederick II of Prussia, 1786

GOOD DOGS

Good King. Bad King.
Depending on which side
of his royal sword you stood on.

Either way, the King's last thought—
    his last chief concern, even
    in the throes of delirium—
was for the warmth of his good dog.

And I call it good, because a book
claims it was his favorite greyhound.

And favorite dogs are good dogs,
even if they are bad sometimes.

We'll huff and shout—*Bad dog!*
even when the bad is barely.

But we know, after all,
more dogs are good
than bad.

            Unlike kings.

Permit me to point out you have made three mistakes
in spelling.

~ Marquis de Favras, 1790

TO CALL A SPADE

I can see the Marquis now,
turning aslant his accusers,
maybe a quick dry glance
out the corner of his eye,
and pointing to the text
in his death warrant.

It is a worthy goal
to remain a smart-ass
in the blotchy face of blind
patriotism and political lunacy.

To know one's time is up,
    that the stupid among us
    will always remain so,
        but that the fight
        has to be fought.

And... so... why not
take one last chance
to call a spade
                ignorant.

One moment more, executioner,
one little moment!

~ Madame du Barry, 1793

HOURGLASS

My friend's words
on his last Sunday—

the last time I ever
saw him sitting upright,
talking, and breathing—

were a few requests for things
he didn't want said at the funeral.

And his tears were the very last
grains of coarse salt and sand
falling through the squeeze
in the hourglass's disregard
for all his final appeals.

His eyes, the sound
of God's ultimate
silence.

Thou wilt shew my head to the people; it is
worth shewing.
~ Georges Jacques Danton, 1794

MADAME GUILLOTINE

If you had read books
and received an education,
or had one or two intelligent
political thoughts in your brain,
the 1700s in France would've been
a good time to get a guillotine speech
all polished up and ready for the big day.
Some tens of thousands got their chance.

The National Razor—a tool designed
to increase the speed in production of
rolling-heads-per-hour—was a staple
there in the City of Enlightenment.

> Maids knitting in their bonnets
> became the first-known version
> of the Dallas Cowboy Cheerleaders.

And I've wondered who among the wise
would speak out, knowing that a date with
Madame Guillotine would be inevitable...

but Monsieur Danton has convinced me
that a good dose of narcissism
might be the key.

I think I could eat one of Bellamy's veal pies.

~ William Pitt the Younger, 1806

In Good Taste

If you have some time left—
maybe an hour, or more—
and an ambulatory companion
willing to pop down to the store
around the corner for a last snack,

what's it gonna be?

Well, it won't be makin's
for a small spring salad
or broccoli casserole
with aloe vera juice.

But a box or three or four
of those Mystic Mint cookies
surely does come to mind—
a shiny mint-chocolate-dipped-
Oreo-type thing from Nabisco,
or one of the other purveyors
of processed, trans-fatty,
white-floured death.

And given time to ponder
that weight is no longer an issue,
a person reels from the onslaught
of sugary and deep-fried possibilities.

I'm just shootin' from the hip here,
but Krispy Kreme's got to be in the mix.
A pitcher of French Roast dark enough
to raise the dead, or at least add on
a few hours to the tail-end of even
the direst of medical conditions.

> I am especially fond
> of the maple-frosted ones.
> (I'm back to the donuts now.)
> Of course, I would add crispy
> bacon crumbles, sprinkled
> generously over the top.

And though I wanted to avoid
the loss of any other animal's life
on the occasion of my mere death,

I'm afraid the gate's been opened now.

> So...
>   once the tequila shows up...

I die happy.

~ Charles James Fox, 1806

To Sing Hallucinated

I suppose I would, die happy,
here among the marked few,
this odd elite crew, the souls
who found that thing they do,
their absurd and holy callings
designed by heaven's own
team of half-crazed angels—
    an assignment accompanied
    by a big black hole sucking
    all hope for remuneration
    back over its dark horizon—
        but an assignment, nonetheless,
        suffused with the deepest shades
        of joy and purpose to be known
        this side of an idle grave. Yes, these
        that Federico García Lorca called

> *strange but simple folk*
> *who sing hallucinated*
> *by a brilliant point of light.*

Yes, these happy hounds
who sink their worn teeth
into that ragged chew-toy
of their divine appointment,
and shake for all they're worth.

Now, why on earth did I do that?

~ Major-General Sir William Erskine, 1813

DECISIONS, DECISIONS

We make decisions.
    Life forces them on us.
We make bad ones and, when lucky,
good ones. Though they are rare.

For some, the bad ones take root at our feet,
then creep up our bodies and into our minds,
manifesting as neck-twitches, hair-pulling,
or sometimes as a violent head-bobbing.

For others, they seep out our lips as muffled
voices we cannot stop from slipping through
the gaps in our gritted and grinding teeth.

And for a few of us, bad decisions go as far
as to turn us into psychopathic hermits—
silent Freudian cowboys out riding the range
and amber waves of our disappointment.

This is why, during some breakdown
along the way, we must make
yet one more decision—

to laugh at ourselves…
or die long before
they bury us.

Don't give up the ship!

~ Captain James Lawrence, 1813

ALL HANDS ON DECK!

I look up to the stars
of my hope for the world
my daughter will sail through
and attempt to keep my eyes
peeled on them up there,
winking just above the deep
jaded stripes of my cynicism—
    the thinking man's favorite
    mask to cover his indolence.

And I know the earth keeps sinking
down in the dark waves of space.
And I know we are the ones
who shot her full of holes.

But look up at Black Mesa
on some cold spring morning,
or to the Sangre de Cristo Range
in the falling shadows of autumn.

See the sun peek over the Atlantic,
or nestle down in the red horizon's
slow burn along the Mediterranean.

Jump and glide along with dolphins
in the blue reaches of the Pacific,
or touch an eagle's back in flight.

Sit still long enough for a finch
to land on your right shoulder,
or maybe for your daughter
to read a book in your lap,

and then tell me...

>   you're ready
>   to surrender.

Do open the shutter in the bedroom,
in order that more light may enter.

~ Goethe, 1832

MORE LIGHT

The morning regulars
lean back in their chairs
around the community table
in the hearth of the Red Cup.

Winter-white sunlight pierces
the back window and explodes
when it hits their mugs and plates,
radiating up into teeth and laughter.

It's "Ellen" this and "Letterman" that.
Then it's "economic tailspin" this
and "children living below
the poverty line" that.
And it's "democrats" this
but definitely "republicans"
that... You know it is...

Soon the talk turns to one of their own,
a regular who didn't survive her last bout
with manic depression after losing mom
and the job with the mortgage company
she'd held for over twenty-five years.

That's when a couple of them
stop to look out the window.

GOD AND TEXAS –
VICTORY OR DEATH!

~ William Barret Travis, 1836

Texas is really four states—
which is an oversimplification.

To West Texans, an East Texan ain't
no gooder than all the other trouble
that come over from Lou'siana.
And besides, they got them
a tree problem over there.

To East Texans, a man from El Paso
might just as well be from Tijuana.

While those up in the North—
as far as the other three states
are concerned—'re just Okies.

And since my in-laws hail
from the South, I'll leave that
alone for now. But, as a whole,
this state's collective psychological
tick, remains that everybody still
talks like William Barret Travis
three days before the Alamo,

seeming to forget...
that everyone died.

I leave this rule for others when I'm dead,
Be always sure you're right, then go ahead.

~ Davy Crockett, 1836

GOING AHEAD

Who among us, Davy,

    from poets and politicians,
    to priests and platoon leaders...

    from Genghis Khan and Gaddafi,
    to Pope Alexander and Henry VIII...

    from every mom at a PTA meeting,
    to every dad yelling at a referee...

    as well as every Hitler who ever
    pulled the genocidal trigger...

Yes, who among us—oh hero
of the ratty coon-skin cap—
ever paused and thought:

    I'm sure I am wrong.

I can hardly breathe; I am suffocating.

~ Alexander Pushkin, 1837

OR MAYBE I WAS THINKING
OF BUKOWSKI

In the throes
of love, death,
or trying to write
the next damn line,
poets revert to dramatic
words like these sometimes
when we realize our metaphors
aren't grabbing anyone's attention.

And Pushkin—just one more poet
to die younger than I'm hoping to—
does have me convinced, nonetheless,
that if I ever hope to gain some notoriety,
or maybe even a readership, for god's sake,

I'm going to need to stride—stark naked—
out from airplane bathrooms now and then,
    piss in more brightly burning fireplaces
    at more upscale Christmas parties
    in much nicer neighborhoods,
        maybe even challenge
        my brother-in-law
        to a duel.

Have You No Bayonets?

~ Sir George Cathcart, 1854

Sometimes
we do not intend
for words to be our last,
necessarily.

It's just that they give us
a pretty good idea
of what's about
to happen.

And that the odds
don't look to be
in our favor.

I am not going to die, am I? He will not separate us,
we have been so happy.

~ Charlotte Brontë, 1855

ALL OF A SUDDEN

I didn't expect
to care this much
about staying alive.

In past relationships,
death hovered out there
in the haze on the horizon
as a potential release.

Now it growls,
creeps up closer,
mutters in my ear
that if I don't get down
and do a damn pushup
or two, get off my ass
and onto that bicycle,
or maybe eat a bit more
broccoli and blueberries,

I'm going to lose the best
heart and pair of hazel eyes
that I am ever going to have
the privilege of not deserving.

GOD WILL PARDON ME;
IT IS HIS TRADE

~ Heinrich Heine, 1856

There are, however, a few
good women who will not

pardon me. And they will
make a point of not doing it.

They will, instead, bring to bear
all within their feminine powers

to block my entry into heaven,
by bargaining with the Devil,

even prevailing upon Mary,
the Mother of God herself,

to get her son's holy father
to reverse his decision.

> The crimes of this guilty land will never be purged
> away but with blood.
>
> ~ John Brown, 1859

SEEING SIGNS

My country raised me well
here in the more laid back
and tall-Indiangrass reaches
of its overlooked heartland.

And we take hearts for granted,
at least until they malfunction—
especially when we live way off
in the fingers and toes of it all.

But I live only a mile or so away
from a main artery that flushes
the used up blood and bygone
sorrows of this great nation.

That's why I would ask you
not to shush me with some
coastal glance of superiority
when I say I have witnessed

more than once this vast land
I love—these United States—
    grab its chest… wince…
    and drop to its knees.

Let us cross over the river and sit under the shade of
the trees.

~ General 'Stonewall' Jackson, 1863

CHRISTMAS GIFT

She loves Christmas,
drags boxes from the attic
well before Thanksgiving Day,
organizing the garlands, tinsel,
and tree ornaments, separating
the tangled strands of icicle lights
from strings of multicolored bulbs.

And then, when the sun goes down
on a late November's Thanksgiving,
her yuletide bells go off like a pistol
at the start of a fifty-meter dash.

A decency glows inside her
that unnerves darker souls,
melting their guns and knives
into much more useful tools.

I have seen her quiet smile
and innocence blow holes
in stonewalled fortresses
twice her size and age.

So here in the soft lull
of this Christmas afternoon,
I owe her and any memory of her
this:

She is my river,

my earthly savior
on this side of it,

and my shade
over on the other.

Texas. Texas! Margaret…

~ Samuel 'Sam' Houston, 1863

Native Sons

What is it
about this crazy
half-cocked state
that makes the men
who fought for her—

  who were born, lived,
  and died in her big bosom,
  who still believe she should
  secede from the Union—

yes, what is it about this place
that makes them cry out for *her*
in the moments of their deaths,

even before the better names
of all those better women
who suffered through
their patriotic lunacy?

They couldn't hit an elephant at this distance.

~ Major-General John Sedgwick, 1864

MY BEST SHOT

The declarative sentence
comes back to haunt us more
than any question we ever ask.

And the enemy shot and killed
General Sedgwick only seconds
after he mocked their abilities.

Yet the declaration remains
such a favorite tool and tack
of most middle school girls
and disgruntled politicians.

Even the poet, Stephen Dunn,
told me in a stanza I just read,
"Life itself is promiscuous."

And within that bawdy claim
he reminded me, that though
the path *is* fraught with danger,

the true poet will eventually be
asked at some point to actually
say something to the people.

She won't think anything about it.

~ Abraham Lincoln, 1865

WAKE UP, BOYS

Men, and our assumptions.
How many of us must die
before we learn that she *will*
think something about it?

Of course, on that night
the President and his wife
were having an uncommonly
good time of it, holding hands
in their box at Ford's Theatre.

And while it's true that he was
speaking of another woman,
another woman they knew,
    (and she wasn't the one
        who shot him)

sometimes I still believe
men were naturally selected
to be terribly slow learners.

Tell mother, I died for my country…

~ John Wilkes Booth, 1865

TELL MOTHER

that I did indeed brush
and floss to the very end,
and that I did not mean
those terrible things I said
in my late teens and early 20s.

Tell her that I always threw out
the salmon after three days,
and that I've unhooked all
the hoses for tonight's freeze
and set the faucets to a slow drip.

Oh, and that I made an appointment
with the gastroenterologist she likes.
      The good one, not the new guy.

Let her know I have backed off
the sauce a bit lately, and that
my drinking is not her fault,
and that I promise to eat my
Brussels sprouts in heaven.

But, most of all, tell her
she did an excellent job
under the circumstances.

I do not have to forgive my enemies,
I have had them all shot.

~ Don Ramón María de Narváez y Campos,
First Duke of Valencia, 1868

TRUTH AND CONSEQUENCES

Remove all consequences, along with any
residual fear that death is not an absolute
molecular end to existence, and there's
no telling what liberties I might take.

I doubt even Gandhi felt no hate
throughout every crawling hour
of his patient and sweaty life.
He just chose a less violent
means of dealing with it all.

And we know that Jesus threw
one fine fit, along with those tables
and chairs, there in his father's temple.

But I don't know that having my enemies
shot would bring the joy and satisfaction
one hopes for upon his demise. And since
I don't feel the numb luxury of certitude
that nothing happens when we die,
I'll forgo this indulgent daydream.

The Duke played his hand.

I'll play mine.

IT IS NO USE

~ General Robert E. Lee, 1870

My daughter poses for her 7th grade picture
with a strangely adult sense of false poise.
Long, immaculate hair. A disarmingly
sweet face. A smile like the Mona Lisa.

But the t-shirt with NIRVANA in pink letters
over Kurt Cobain's sunglassed face, flashes hot
like a pistol shot, reminding me she was leaning
forward in her race to the tape of a 13th birthday.

And her eyes tell me that even then she knew
war is wrong. Even when launched for God.
Even when financial experts drum one up
for the sake of the American economy.
And even when we fight it so cleanly
and technologically that none of ours
are lost in the cause for petroleum.

A few poems ago I led you to believe
the last words out of the rasping lips
of the actor John Wilkes Booth were
Tell mother, I died for my country…

Actually, there was one more…
and he felt the need to repeat it.

Useless… Useless…

QUIÉN ES? QUIÉN ES?
WHO IS IT? WHO IS IT?

~ Billy the Kid, 1881

He never saw it comin'.

A dark room.
Two shots fired.

But a lifetime of dishing it out
usually ends in taking the same.

Like the day that'll soon come
when some fresh young buck
will write the flashier words
that render most of mine
outdated and irrelevant.

It's simply the nature
and biology of it all.

I just hope it takes
more than two bullets
to bring me down.

I must go in, the fog is rising.

~ Emily Dickinson, 1886

THE BETTER POET

The good poet
may leave us with
some enigmatic gem
to hold up in the glow
of a swinging light bulb.

No intimation as to what
she might have meant.

But the better poet
leaves us dying
to know what
it means
to us.

The most skillful gambler and nerviest, speediest,
deadliest man with a six-gun I ever knew.

~ Wyatt Earp remembering
John Henry 'Doc' Holliday, 1887

WHAT'S AT STAKE

I have seen severe talent,
those with a certain head-on gift.

I've seen a couple of them die without
the recognition they deserved—at least
as much as those on any bestseller list,
or Hollywood's well-rehearsed minions
standing with smiles and arms uplifted
in the deadening glow of the spotlight.

Reality television should embarrass us
collectively as a devolving species.
It slates us for early extinction.
Its stars are all reputation
without cogitation—
all special-guest-on-talk-show
with little more than a forefinger
twisting starched hair during a few
Oh my goshes here, and one or two
Like, you knows thrown in there.

Yet there are those of rare birth
who owned their reputations,
like Kerouac's "mad ones"
who "burn, burn, burn."

The ones left standing, pistol
already back inside the holster
when the blue smoke clears.

Doc Holliday had the reputation
of total badass because he was
a total badass—a reputation
I have not earned because
I'm too attached to living.

But I run the numbers every day,
and think about what it would take
to solve the sad and wimpy situation.

And I just now drained a shot glass full
of Herradura Double Barrel Reposado
and slammed it down on the table
as if I damn well mean
to do something
about it.

HURRAH FOR ANARCHY!

~ George Engel, 1887

As with habanero peppers
and the splitting of atoms,
a small amount of anarchy
seems to go a long way.

Hippies and artists,
two similar beasts with
varying degrees of hygiene,
move where the rental rates
are a last resort of desperate
downtown property owners.

Soon though, after several
massive and colorful murals
have appeared on the sides
of brown brick buildings,
one of the hippies opens up
a funky coffee shop and posts
that Thursday nights will be

OPEN MIC NIGHT

The beginning of every end.

If that goes well, another hippie—
often one who went to a big school
somewhere on a coast—gets a loan
for a little backlit organic restaurant
and calls up his old college roommate
who happens to be a CIA-trained chef

that happens to be sick of her successful
restaurant in Manhattan's Upper West,
and before you catch the whole mess
by its great-big-old rusted zipper,
some well-known poet moves in
because he's tired of Santa Fe.

And right about that point—
or at least not too long after—
a Walgreens, a nice Trader Joe's,
and a couple of Starbucks pop up,

and you can pretty much
    close the velvet curtains
        and pack the U-Haul.

THE SADNESS WILL LAST FOREVER

~ Vincent Van Gogh, 1890

Some years,
and for some hearts,
the spring doesn't redeem
all the lost colors of winter.

The chemically stable among us
don't get that smoothies, jogging,
and a good therapist do not cure
all that ails and tortures.

And so it was,
    at some point,
a sad synaptic thing
pulled down the shades
on Van Gogh's dying sun

    and pushed him
    to paint the moon

        and all those stars
        in the darkness.

I am not going. Do with me what you like.

~ Sitting Bull, 1890

I AM NOT GOING

As I shuffled my way through
the day's pieces of mail I saw
that I'd been invited to join
the American Association
of Retired Persons
and hissed,

Hey, dammit. I'm only 46.
Get your records in order.

And when no one heard me,
those last words of Sitting Bull
became a soiled flag I picked up
out of the mud on the battlefield,

raising it up as high as I could
and running with it headlong
into the smoke and flames
of the very near future.

What's that? Do I look strange?

~ Robert Lewis Stevenson, 1894

FOLLOWING THE NEWS

The ever-presence
of clean mirrors remains
a true source of at least one
key psychological benefit
to the human's fragile
and sacred vanity:

> they allow us
> to track and trace
> our epidermal demise
> with such a daily consistency

>> that our eventual derangement
>> becomes almost imperceptible.

I am dying as I have lived:
beyond my means.

~ Oscar Wilde, 1900

LIVING BEYOND

It seems dying
beyond one's means
would be much easier
than living beyond them.

Obnoxious bill collectors,
hellishly persistent as the are,
are not likely to follow you
where you are going. And

not even divorce lawyers
can track down that
private number.

It's a long time since I drank champagne.

~ Anton Chekhov, 1904

I'VE MADE MY BED,
NOW I'LL DRINK IN IT

The only thing worse than
having life shortened by a few
good years from drinking
too much champagne,

would be to have it
lengthened by a few
boring years without it.

ON THE CONTRARY!

~ Henrik Johan Ibsen, 1906

My friend had written
for enough years now
to begin to disagree
with his previous self.

So when a fan brought up
an old poem at the Q & A,
he launched into an internal
fray with his estranged ego,
while still managing to make
the audience believe somehow
that he was speaking to them.

And it went on for a while,
until the last little thread
snapped on the button
that held his relative
decorum in check.

He is now holed up inside
a log cabin deep in some dark
woods out west, I have heard,
working on innovative ways
to finally escape himself.

I think I could forget all the wrongs that I have ever
received…
                                    ~ Geronimo, Goyathlay, 1909

IF

"If…" That's the word, the next part
we do not hear him explain, nor did we
honor back when he tried to explain it.

Geronimo wanted to take his people back
from Oklahoma to die in some sort of peace,
albeit a sad one, in his native land of Arizona.

Very much the way I will feel for Oklahoma
if I stay here in Texas where I was born—
my family and I living in exile at the time.

I mean no slight to my few Texan friends
who will want to stay, die and be buried here
with the same passion—a passion someone

from Hell's Kitchen, or East St. Louis,
or the end of Hollywood Boulevard,
may or may not understand too well.

But the callused brown toes and bloody
overworked fingers of my ancestors
dug in deep and hard to the scorched

red dirt of Oklahoma's wide, stoic plains.
And thick roots like those are absolute hell
to get down to and pull out of the ground.

My sun is set. My day is done.
Darkness is stealing over me.

~ Chief Red Cloud, 1909

A DARK BREW

I am at the end of having done
everything I was allowed to do
in the raising of my daughter.
My ex may think I'm talking
about money, and disagree.

But my beautiful assignment
will be driving within months,
dancing in the dangerous arms
of all that she believes is now
hers to decide. And I see red
clouds on the dark horizons
of her eyes as the night falls
on my sad, limited influence.
Her cynicism glints like a razor
in moonlight. Her certainty,
as deadly as mine almost was.

I don't know what will carry her
through to a truer dream
and desire to live.

But I doubt the gods,
    demons that they are,
        will allow it to be me.

Death, the only immortal, who treats us alike…

~ Mark Twain, 1910

FAIR'S FAIR

Something makes me smile
when I think Donald Trump
himself, will not even be able
to buy his way out of this one.

The richest man in the world,
give or take a few multi-billionaires,
may find a way to lengthen it artificially,
but he'll only begin to look as bad
as his hair already does.

In death, the mighty
disintegrate into parodies.

And the poets, sometimes,
rise up…   finally heard.

Not that death is disinterested.

Just, in the end, fair.
And firm about it.

I AM VERY GLAD

~ King Edward VII, the "Uncle of Europe," 1910

Glad that Yellowstone's caldera,
brooding beneath the beautiful park,
did not finally blow a moon-sized crater
in the planet's blue and green face today...
    and that some people still read books.

Glad that those who are angry with God
for not annihilating the infidels for them,
did not find the red switch on the side
of the green nuclear warhead today...
    and that the blue agave still grows
    in the high plains of Mexico.

Glad that the asteroids have,
so far at least, passed us by...
    and that most governors
    in the U.S. have term limits.

Glad that Paris still lights up at night...
    and that my teenager actually smiled
    at something I said the other day...
      and that humans evolved enough
      to develop and perfect the recipe
      for Mint Chocolate Chip ice cream.

Turn up the lights; I don't want to go home
in the dark.

~ O. Henry, 1910

BREATHE AGAIN

Do we meet our child self
in the hallway on the way out?
Does it take our tired, shaking hands
and laugh at how silly we look, old, afraid?

What floods back in?
Maybe the vague memory
of how to breathe correctly—
that thing we only ever knew how
to do in the very first hours of our lives?

O. Henry was quoting a song by Harry Williams.
But some synaptic wisp brought the lines
back to his mind in those last minutes.

I'm living long enough to appreciate
that I lost a few things that matter
way back in those earlier years.

And, crazy as it may be,
I'm hoping that death
is a chance to go
retrieve them.

For God's Sake Look After
Our People

~ Captain Robert Falcon Scott, 1912

I imagine a random sample
of congressmen assembled
against their blue-blood wills
in a quiet location of my choice.

None of them are able to speak—
which would never happen of course
without stuffing a sock into every mouth.

What would I say to them?
How would I say it,
there at my end?

I need more time
to think this over,
but, for my tastes,
Captain Scott was
much too polite.

Ladies, you are next...
hold that boat.

~ Colonel John Jacob Astor IV, 1912

ABANDON THEORY!

I am a vain and selfish man who's still afraid of
death. And I came close to writing a poem revealing
that I am not a fourth the man Colonel Astor was.
That I would have "tripped" and "fallen" into the
lifeboat bearing my pregnant wife down to the North
Atlantic, then apologized for my clumsiness to the
two nice ladies left on deck. But then, I began to
doubt my disbelief in myself, thinking I might at least
be three-fourths the man and would've helped them
in spite of my weakness.

So I abandoned that theory and turned to prose
instead in order to focus on two academically-
empowered women that I remember from a few
interminable semesters in grad school. They despised
my Y-chromosomal endowment by virtue of its
existence, spending angry amounts of class-time
denouncing my genetic heritage and, in short,
blaming my penis for the sins of all penises
throughout the history of womankind.

What could I say? Men are low-functioning
vertebrates with little understanding of how their
hormones affect the other children on the
playground?

Yet, as the light dims on those memories, it turns out this exercise is more about my desire, albeit vain and selfish, to put these two wraiths back there on the deck of the Titanic, in place of the two ladies who accepted Colonel Astor's incredibly chauvinistic offer, and maybe catch their reaction to such a gender-biased situation.

If they had turned it down, giving him the same tiresome lectures they gave me, at the same ridiculous volume, I would've stood up—from my seat in the lifeboat, of course—and saluted them, fingers on forehead.

But if they had accepted, and allowed him to lower them through the open porthole, I would've shoved them out of the lifeboat, straight down into the icy waves, and told the Colonel:

Get on in, my good man!
That's the last of 'em!

As to me, I leave here tomorrow for an unknown
destination.

~ Ambrose Bierce, Circa 1914

TAKE A BOW

At 71, Mister Bierce drew the curtains,
excused himself from the United States,
and then wrote a letter to his niece
that he'd rather be "shot to rags"
in Mexico than trip and fall
"down the cellar stairs."

And I wonder what responsible
favor I might do my wife some day,
as well as whatever few straggling
friends choose to stick around.

It's nothing to do with my age,
though I am reproachable there.

No, just a concern, we could say,
over the unnerving possibility
of coming to be known so well
by the ones you love so much,
that they now stand next to you
at parties and on holidays only
out of a sense of obligation...
or a commitment she made...
fetching your tequila for you
because it makes you easier
to tolerate. Maybe even
a little funnier at times.

I die like a true blue rebel.
Don't waste any time in mourning.

~ Joe Hill, 1915

FIRE!

Once convicted, the citizens of
Salt Lake City gave him a choice:
hanging — or the firing squad.

And when he heard the voice
shout *Ready!* and then *Aim!*
his very last word was...
actually...
                    Fire!

And so it is I've been letting
my sixteen-year-old daughter
drive us up to her high school
during rush-hour this week.

   She is so excited about
   her brand new permit.

I have made my choice.

   I'm ready to ride.

IT IS UNBELIEVABLE

~ Mata Hari, 1917

It *is*
unbelievable,
I suppose.

Gravity...
that we adhere
to a carbon ball.

The immediacy of bias
in the news, a blueberry's
power to stain cement.

Birth, the popularity
of reality television,
the Kardashians.

Styrofoam,
aerodynamics,
congress, pork.

That coffee one day
met up with cream,
my daughter singing.

Fermentation, and that
    Mata Hari blew a kiss
        to her firing squad.

I am the enemy you killed, my friend.

~ Wilfred Owen, 1918

HERETIC THAT I AM

You exercise good intentions,
   and a python-like death grip
   on the hard-to-swallow list
   of things that irritate God,
to now squeeze me into some
doghouse of the backslidden.

About 2,000 years ago you simply
would have stoned or crucified me.
500, and you would've burned me
at the stake. Or drowned me
in the nearest farm pond.

Unorthodox interpretation
and schismatic questioning
were easier to quell back then.
The solutions…   more final.

And it still bugs you to no end
that Jesus and I have much more
in common… that if he returned,
he'd probably come to my house
first, for margaritas and cheese…
maybe a little somethin' to help him
get through one of your interminable
services of praise songs and a pep talk.

But I also know that chaos
is one hard egg to swallow,
and that you are just trying
to bring some moral decency
and a better wallpaper pattern
to the disarray of the universe.

But, I would appreciate it
if you would take me off
your long and holy list
of stuff to worry about.

Whatever happens, my fellow-countrymen
won't kill me.
~ Michael "Mick" Collins, 1922

BUT EVERYBODY LOVES *ME*

I have overestimated
my likeability as well.

For forty-six years
I made the mistake

of lending credibility
to mother's opinion.

And now I can't,
for the life of me,

imagine that anyone
might actually want

me
out of the picture.

Take a step forwards, lads.
It will be easier that way.

~ Erskine Childers, 1922

SMALL GESTURES

Right before
they tie the blindfold
and then fire the final shots...

... to blow a Marilyn Monroe kiss from
the balcony down to the U.S. Senate,
just before showing them my ass.

... to streak, between sessions,
through the annual conference
of the Southern Baptist Convention.

... to lick a terrorist on the cheek
while he tries on his newly-
rigged vest in the basement.

... to simultaneously submit
this poem to *The Harvard,
Paris,* and *Kenyon Reviews.*

... then to pump Pavarotti's version
of Puccini's "Nessun dorma!"
through the loud speakers,

     as I smile and wink
     at my trembling
     executioners.

Don't let it end like this.
Tell them I said something.

~ Pancho Villa, 1923

THE WORLD IS WAITING...

It's so haunting, so sad,
that desperate moment
when we realize too late
we should've read books.

We thought our notoriety,
a sort of fame, and the fear
we'd inspired across the land,
would speak for us in the end.

That loved ones would weep,
alongside compadres and fans,
and that we might be engulfed
by the poor we'd championed.

It just never crossed our minds
that the press and the paparazzi
would swoop down like vultures
for the last gasp and final breath.

That's good. Go on, read some more.

~ President Warren G. Harding, 1923

WHAT LITTLE TIME

I miss it...
       that time...
when I could read her to sleep.
Those years when she wouldn't
enter the land of nod without it.

Now she texts herself to sleep,
alone in her room, lights out
and under the covers, while I
read myself into restlessness
in my threadbare recliner.

       And I wonder,
if the time were to come
when I couldn't anymore,
for the sake of lost sight,

       if she might be willing.

... my last request: Everything I leave behind me ... in the way of diaries, manuscripts, letters ... sketches, and so on, [is] to be burned unread.

~ Franz Kafka, 1924

ON THE STUDY OF GESTURES

Some final expressions are acts
of a conscientious humility.
Or maybe a genuine fear
that what we've done
is not any good.

Others are deeds of
aggrandizing selfishness.
Empty gestures we make
to those who try to love us.

This one came from a man
who saw death as a stepping
off into "a roaring nothing."
And that writing might be
the only thing worse.

At least Kafka's friends
ignored his last request.

(Which begins our course on ethics...)

BECAUSE IT IS THERE

~ George Mallory, 1924

I wasted years explaining
all the Everests of my life
to people who don't care for
mountain climbing that much.

They prefer to glance at peaks
on covers of coffee-table books
and then download them later if
something appeals to their tastes.

They love the stories of the few
who have made it to the top.
But they don't want to see
anyone they're related to
throw away his life, time,
and money by pursuing
such impractical elevations.

So, I do my best to keep
all my long-term plans—
calculations and itineraries—
to myself, knowing that nobody
really cares, yet that they might
be proud of me if I reached
the summit someday.

Don't worry, Chief, I will be all right.

~ Rudolph Valentino, 1926

I'LL BE FINE

The early morning sun blinds me
as I head north on I-25. The sharp
and crystalline peaks of snow-capped
Sangre de Cristos cut through God's
dark blue flesh here where he bleeds
all over these scrubby foothills.

The sight of it sends a shock
of electric joy along my spine,
causes a swelling in my throat,
a throbbing yet cautious desire.

All the symptoms I've experienced
before over the forty years I've come
to the high desert plains of New Mexico.

It's electric because of the searing altitude
and stunning desolation. And I'm cautious
because it makes me want to move here.

I have learned to be wary of the world's
geographic supermodels. The way they
suck you in and clean out your wallet,
then leave you sleeping on a bench
in the plaza, trying to figure out
a way to get back home.

I'm tired of fighting, Dash.
I guess this thing is going to get me.

~ Harry Houdini, 1926

THE GOOD FIGHT

For some, death
is a much needed rest,
a final break in the game.

They lived in such a way...
    or maybe to the extent...
that dying now makes sense.

It's just a last, good, stiff drink
they drain then slam on the bar
at the end of a life's hard work.

Too many of us hoard our lives
instead, while these rare few
are out spending theirs.

Farewell, my friends. I go to glory!

~ Isadora Duncan, 1927

A FRIEND... OR SOMEONE

At times I wonder how many
of the glamorously notorious
did not say as they were dying
what they are said to have said

but were "saved," let's say,
by a friend... or someone
who had a better idea for
what should've been said.

For example, *I go to glory!*

    versus

I go now to have sex in a hotel room
with a sexy French-Italian mechanic!

which, it turns out, is much closer
to what Ms. Duncan had said. And so,

I hope a good friend... or someone
with a better idea and tongue...
will do the same for me.

You stick to your trade
I'll stick to mine.

~ Arnold 'The Brain' Rothstein, 1928

OUR ASSIGNMENTS

I will go ahead and leave
the running of the country
to the good men and women
who believe that can be done.

The men and women who have
the money to buy the sharp suits
they love to wear to do the work.

The ones who've had the elective
surgery for conscience removal,
so they can do it to our faces.

And I'll stick to writing
about them.

Nothing's so sacred as honor
and nothing's so loyal as love.

~ Epitaph on Wyatt Earp's tombstone, 1929

So, What's the Story?

Whose life these days,
with the way Americans
tends to live it now, will
arrive at the tail of its end
worthy of becoming a story?

What pale-face, buried
in his glowing notepad,
could be in danger at all
of becoming interesting
to future generations—

    his fingers twiddling
    at the virtual keypad,
        instead of twitching
        at the blue steel trigger
        of a Colt .45 Peacemaker?

When solid stock options
mean more than our honor…
when every day we forfeit love
for ESPN and Saks Fifth Avenue…
    where do we go from there?

And who among our grandchildren will care?

It Is Very Beautiful over There!

~ Thomas Alva Edison, 1931

The old saying tells us
not to look over where
the grass is always greener.
It makes itself quite clear.

But I've paused for a spell,
and since I'm standing here,
I simply cannot help myself.
It is impossible not to stare.

I mean, look at it for yourself
and then tell me you don't care.
Tell me you do not see it too...
that it is so beautiful over there!

If this is dying, I don't think much of it.

~ Giles Lytton Strachey, 1932

MY SENTIMENT

Only God can get men
energized about dying.

Even the ones with big
orange prescription vials

or pistol barrels sealed
between quivering lips,

approach it with a certain
hesitancy, or with alcohol.

As for me, I do grow weary
of day to day living at times,

and I have watched disease
turn it into day to day dying,

but I've never, not once,
gotten tired of life.

I feel I am no longer fit in these times.

~ John Calvin Coolidge, 1933

ANACHRONISM

I hit that plateau in 7th grade.
Right around the time I realized
middle school wouldn't be different
than elementary, and that the silliness
would, most likely, go on and on.

Computers never did thrill me
the way they did all my friends.
I got a cell phone ten years after
they made the magic technology
available to the general public.
I still consider it a ball and chain.

I'll admit though to a funky decade
with synthesizers and drum machines
back in the 1980s, when I was briefly
fascinated by the way they perfected
the rough edges of Caucasian timing.

But alas mine was a soul built by a tired,
old, possibly Chinese engineer who wrote
poems by green tea and dying candlelight.
A soul that was designed for remote cabins
and island shacks. A soul that is—for all
practical 21st Century purposes—useless.

God damn you!

~ King George V, 1936

ONE WHO HERE IN WHOVILLE

I can think of only one person—
one who has not murdered children,
a certain who that I knew too well—
to whom I might want to offer
these as my very last words.

For those who murder children,
there are no words. Therefore, they
should only be spoken by death itself.

As for that certain who for whom
I reserve King George's final words,
I'm not allowed to say, sadly, who
this who is… for legal reasons.

But I can tell you there will be
more than one who who thinks
this certain who is him… or her.

As for these sorry whos in my life
who don't *quite* deserve these words,
they may feel a slight disappointment,
when in the end I decide not to bother.

Listen folks; I'm gonna have to stop for a minute,
because I've lost my voice. This is the worst thing I've
ever witnessed.

~ Herb Morrison
on the Hindenburg Disaster, May 6th, 1937

MR. MORRISON AND ME

I can't top Mr. Morrison, or
the black and white footage
of that blimp, it's skin slowly
burning away. The screams
still chill me to the bone.

I mean no disrespect, but...
I don't do well with actual death.
I've gotten too close once or twice.

And, like I was saying, I can't top
the Hindenburg. I've only seen
what I've seen in my 46 years,
like the Bush administration,
or the national news coverage
of wars fought in God's name,
or my friend slowly destroyed
one cancerous cell at a time.

Still... I do understand
Mr. Morrison's need
to just stop talking
there at the end.

Goodbye, I'll see you in heaven.

~ John D. Rockefeller, 1937

GOOD FOR HIM

I'm not sure I trust any man
who glides out on the greasy
cogs of a cliché like that one.

Though I imagine it was easier
for an old billionaire who owned
most of the East Coast to believe
in heaven. He'd likely laid down
a healthy deposit ahead of time
to secure his smooth ride on in,
as well as some damn fine digs
fully furnished upon his arrival.

I don't doubt the insane power
of gross wealth. Not anymore.
Not now that I've watched it
chew up the green forests,
gold plains, and blue hills
of my daughter's future
and spit them out into
the wheezing oceans.

We must be on you, but cannot see you –
but gas is running low…

~ Amelia Earhart, 1937

AT 1,000 FEET

To fly in a small aircraft,
the Lockheed Electra of
rapidly diminishing odds,
on instruments only now,

the ship there to guide you
but unable to communicate
on your one good frequency
as you dream about nothing,

other than that mile-long
island in the foggy Pacific,

is to fly in the foreknowledge
of so much salt and darkness,
and the sad gauge's inability
to register fuel indefinitely,

while the beach you believe
exists in the scattered clouds
and deep shadows up ahead
may…   never be found.

Now it is nothing but torture and makes no sense
anymore.
~ Sigmund Freud, 1939

PAVLOV'S MAN

He suffered outrageous
pain there in his last days—
probably from thirty or more
operations he'd had on his jaw
to deal with tumors that were
from the twenty or so cigars
he smoked every single day.

(Or the tumors might've been
from a generation of mothers
seeking psychic revenge for how
he had ruined their relationships
with all their middle-aged sons.)

But he'd been an intelligent man,
with far too much time to think
about our collective psychosis,
who had chosen to dance
with the Pavlovian habit
that took him down.

I am only asking for one thing –
let me finish my work.

~ Isaac Babel, 1940

LET ME FINISH

My narrative-poet friend
had a knock-down drag-out
with two imagists one night.

Pummeled 'em over pinball
in a bar with the beautiful
fists of Elizabeth Bishop.

They were all flash and bells,
quick on feet and metaphors,
and therefore no match at all

for his epic hook at the *beginning*
and classic uppercuts in the *middle*,
or the standing 8-count at the *end*...

the only three things a narrative poet
is asking for—a place to start, some-
where to go, and the chance to finish.

I don't want them to undress me.
I want you to do it.

~ Leon Trotsky, 1940

The Ones Who Take Us Under

Best not to think about them
too much. The ones who apply
the makeup, for better or worse,
while families are back at houses
where spouses take sporadic calls.

Kids crying. Brothers and sisters
sad—sisters-in-law, not so much.
Grandkids, sad too, but still eating
the peach pie that the sweet old lady
from the end of street brought over.

No, don't think too much about them,
the morticians who repeat cadaver jokes
at their annual conventions in Boca Raton.

Yes, Florida, because that is where most
of them live. Boca Raton, because that
is where most of their business dies.

And at these conventions they gossip
about our genitalia, or that exceptional
mole on the left buttock, and about
those of us who did not receive
enough notice ahead of time
to clean our toenails and
change our underwear.

And like all the rest of us,
they either do, or do not,
like their quiet, morbid jobs.

But they remain, nonetheless,
our travel agents to the other side.
They undress us, deveil us, take
that last unpowdered look.

And like I said, it's best not
to think about them too much.

I SHOULD NOT FEAR
THE HISTORIAN'S VERDICT

~ Arthur Neville Chamberlain, 1940

Though I worry sometimes
I will not be offensive enough
to catch the historian's attention.
That my words might lack a certain
honesty. And I don't mean the type
that simply makes my mom wonder
where she went wrong. I mean more
an honesty honest enough to offend
ancestors, or to concern a President,
or inspire the murderous indignation
of entire terrorist networks by claiming
that Allah has spoken to me and told me
to tell them to take a Goddamned day off.
That he wants them to sit their overheated
asses down and shut their accursed mouths
long enough for him to get his own word in.
You know... an honesty more like that.
Even if it's not true. I mean, come on,
Allah has never spoken to me. But,
he hasn't spoken to them either.
He's too divinely depressed...
too disappointed... wondering,
like mom, where he went wrong.

So we beat on, boats against the current,
borne back ceaselessly into the past.

> ~ F. Scott Fitzgerald, 1940
> (last words in *The Great Gatsby*)

TROUBLED HEARTS AND LIVERS

Some truths beat too hard
against the walls of our brains.

They are what they are,
as this one is what it is.

No need to rewrite Fitzgerald.
Though, he'd likely think so.

In 1925 came the second printing
of *The Great Gatsby* (three thousand

of them) followed by tuberculosis,
cirrhosis and, finally, the heart.

He died with all the unsold
copies stashed somewhere

in a friend's apartment
in West Hollywood.

DOES NOBODY UNDERSTAND?

~ James Joyce, 1941

For a writer—at least one
serious enough to make life
difficult for his entire family—

it's not hard to feel the muscles
giving way, or the bones breaking,
beneath the weight of these words.

And then to have Ireland refuse
the return of his remains—exiled
from the homeland, even in death.

The reason his ghost still paces back
and forth out in front of Shakespeare
and Company, along the River Seine.

Oh! I have slipped the surly bonds of Earth.

~ John Gillespie Magee, Jr., 1941

SHREDS

One man's thrill
is another's reminder
that death is often as near
as the next bolt of lightning,

or maybe some migrating flock
of Canadian Geese sucked into
and mulched by the hot laughter
and silver teeth of jet propulsion.

When my traveling forces me—
    and force is the word—to fly,
my midair powdered-coffee poems
tend to read like sensible epitaphs,

insufferable little shreds of lyric
I hope a good soul will find
among the debris.

WE MUST KNOW. WE WILL KNOW.

~ David Hilbert, 1943

And we do know, now.
And though there's still more
to know, you couldn't have imagined
what all of this knowing would do to us.

Computers once the size of oil refineries
are now as small as billfolds. And soon,
they will be invisible to the human eye.

We have planes that fly without pilots.
Tiny planes that take out all the trash
and the terror suspects of the world.

Just taste the genetically modified
corn, the individually packaged
energy bars and the Big Macs.

Our food now, more an act
of hard science than a result
of sunshine and a good hoe.

WHAT HAVE I LIVED FOR?

~ Larry Hart, 1943

Some twenty-five years ago,
my answer would've been swift
and peppered with shining crosses,
God's grace, and absolute confidence.

A decade down the road though, divorce
and a lot of reading complicated that grace,
and the crosses began to show some wear.

By that point, I would have likely claimed
I lived for my daughter. But she turns
sixteen soon and has already hit
the open road of her heart.

So, all I've got at the moment
is that I've lived for little more than
the reason that eons ago, space-trash
somehow congealed into carbon balls
that wheel and spin around gaseous stars,
and when oxygen entered the show,
molecular biology and cell division
simply couldn't help themselves,
which then led to the problem
that evolution just could not
keep its hands out of its pants.

A BULLET STOPPED HIS SONG

~ Alun Lewis, 1944

A bullet... or a bottle...
or maybe a bad microbe
teaching T cells to dance
over on their darker side.

Whatever it turns out to be,
statistics tell us that poets
tend to step in front of it,
or off of it... or into it,
a bit sooner than most.

It's a short-haul profession.
It's the poem out of necessity
with lifespans like ours... since
we would never finish a novel.

If only there were no other people in the world.

~ Anne Frank, 1945
the last entry in her diary

AS OUR HONORED GUEST

Dearest Anne,

I have a small group of rude friends,
a loose affiliation of artists, teachers
and ex-cons, who call themselves:
The Brunch for Misanthropes Society.

And though we shun most,
and merely tolerate others—

> those who milk the cows
> for our fine white cheeses,
>   our mothers who bake
>   exquisite pies and breads—

we would have welcomed you
to our heart o' Texas shindigs.

For in your diary you suggest
you had wanted to be a writer.
And judging by your last entry,
I'd say you were on your way.

BE CAREFUL
~ Franklin D. Roosevelt, 1945

My Dear Sierra,

these are the last words that this President
of the United States mumbled to his daughter.

    And since the 21st Century has blessed you
    with every technological means to ensure
    the silent inurement of our relationship,

    and since the smoke and clouds
    of this cultural malaise never clear
    long enough to restore a sense of decency
    to those in charge of the buttons and switches,

    and since my outright refusal to participate
    in the Great American Orgy of Disconnection
    has rendered me terminally uncool in your eyes,

I guess I'll leave you with these two words
from FDR. And add, maybe—*I love you.*

Shakespeare, Here I Come!

~ Theodore Dreiser, 1945

MY DOUBLE-SHOT HEAVEN

My heaven,
as if I'd get to choose,
would be an old coffeehouse
with worn out wooden floors,
full of regulars puffing on pipes
'cause it doesn't matter anymore.

Mark Twain, a regular there,
might be arguing with Gandhi,
and would shout "Poppycock!"
at some point in the conversation.

F. Scott Fitzgerald would sit
in the dark, rubbing his temples
at a back corner table with friends,
still worried that Zelda'll come in
and find him having a good time.

And Gertrude Stein would set foot,
hoping to be seen, though still quite
displeased with everyone's behavior,
particularly Hemingway and Bukowski.

But Old Buk wouldn't give a damn,
never having cared for the ex-pats.
He'd be by the window in boxers

and black boots, pouring whiskey
in his coffee, bitching about Paris
and New York with Louis Céline.

Who knows, Shakespeare himself
might even walk in at some point.
Everyone would shout out *Hey!*
with a raised hand... but then
roll their eyes at each other
while he orders his skinny
vanilla latte with a flourish.

I should have drunk more champagne.

~ John Maynard Keynes, 1946

APOSTASY

My friend unpacked the slotted box
of craft beer and top-shelf liquor
he'd brought to our party. And,
as he pulled out a bottle of tequila,
he spied the professionally-printed
note on cardstock that someone
had hidden underneath it:

> GOD REALLY DOES
> FORGIVE YOU
>
> GET TO KNOW HIM

My buddy choked with laughter,
loved its timing, handed it to me,
his head shaking back and forth
over a past that had to do with
religion and being born in Texas.

The retired-preacher's-kid corner
of my disjointed soul looked at it
long and hard. I paused in silence,
till my shoulders shook, and thought:

Nope... There it is... They start out
by knowing exactly what God does
and doesn't do, somehow. Then...

they throw out some patronizing
and platitudinal commandment.

And in a grand act of autoerotic,
guerilla proselytizing, they drop it
into some place, a dark and musty
space inhabited only by us sinners,
knowing they've done God's work.

So I popped the cork on the tequila
and poured the two of us a stiff one.

Just a little something to warm us
as we stood there in the bitter
cold breeze of theology.

OH GOD

~ Mohandas Gandhi, 1948

To hold your head high,
stare straight into the verdict
of their unsteadied gun barrels...

    to say, I will not fight you,
    but I'll not move from here...

        to watch a mist of confusion
        creep along the blue steel shafts
        until it reaches their gutless fingers...

            and to see the cracked eggshells
            of their bloodshot eyes go wide,
            begin to twitch in the sockets
            of their hot anemic faces,

as the realization wraps around
their throats, that they will lose
on both sides of this trigger.

It is tasteless to prolong life artificially.
I have done my share, it is time to go.

~ Albert Einstein, 1955

THE REST OF US

Einstein peaked as a scientist
in his mid twenties they say,
brought us his best theories
on what energy was equal to,
bending hard time and space
with his brain and bare hands.

As a poet—at almost fifty—
though I sort of understand
the subtle difference between
simile, metaphor, and analogy,

I'm only now beginning to grasp
what enjambment is all about, or
that to scan verse doesn't mean
to view it from a great distance
with a hand shading my eyes.

So… considering how slow
I've been on the uptake in life,
I'm asking that my loved ones
not pull the plug… just yet.

Oh God, here I go.

~ 'Madcap Maxie' Max Baer, 1959

Too Late Now

A good, comfortable
middle-class upbringing...
that is what I have to blame.

Parents who gave me everything
that a teenager needs to survive,
which, in truth, is so much more
than a teenager needs to survive.

A lack of any lack of anything was
my inoculation against good sense,
the condition that sent me whistling
on my way, a guitar on one shoulder,
a journal in a backpack on the other,
as I walked smack into the open jaws
of the lowest and least profitable
branch of all the literary arts.

You made one mistake. You married me.

~ Brendan Francis Behan, 1964

BUT SERIOUSLY,

I joke with my wife
about this all the time.

She laughs… usually.
Sometimes just smiles.

She's tall. Thin. All muscle.
An animal lover. Still hopeful.

And so beautiful that sometimes
I am embarrassed to stand close
to her in big crowds of people
I don't know. And, like I said,

I joke with her about this, but
sometimes I want to lean in
closer and say, *Babe,*
I'm not kidding.

EXCUSE MY DUST

> ~ Dorothy Parker (one of *her* epitaphs), 1967

Larry McMurtry tells the story
of a German farmer who milked
all his dairy cows before going out
to a fresh spread of hay in the barn
and splitting his lips with a 12-gauge.
    He didn't want them to suffer.

And I cannot bear the thought
of one day becoming a hacking,
gagging bag of sodium chloride
in some gray-tiled hospital room,

a sad sack of gas who can't control
his burps and farts in front of nurses
or his loved ones if they come to visit.

Native Americans *walked to the mountain.*
Do they still do that? The Samurai have
that special knife tucked in their sashes.

I keep believing there's a better way.
And not dying at all, of course,
is a favorite of the few plans
I've toyed with so far.

I am just turning 40 and taking my time about it.

~ Harold Lloyd, (at 77) 1971

Makes No Sense

Not too long ago, I sucked in
my belly and stuck out my chest

and boasted on a 40th birthday
that I was... just fine with it,

and that I felt maybe the 40s
would be my golden decade.

That was only yesterday,
but somehow I managed

to turn 47 three, or was it
maybe five or six, days ago.

And if my math bothers you,
imagine how confused I am by it.

Dear World, I am leaving because I am bored.

~ George Sanders, 1972

STUFF TO DO

Boredom's a good reason to leave.
Though, as for me, I can't imagine
stumbling into that sad territory
on such a permanent basis.

No. Boredom for me lasts
only as long as that dinner
at the film professor's house,

> or a "tour of the new facilities,"

>> or the endless poetry reading
>> of a prize-winning novelist.

But always, and never soon enough,
I get back to my crazy, insatiable love
for this mad planet, limping in its orbit.

I'm Going into the Bathroom to Read

~ Elvis Presley, 1977

An artist's soul burns up
in the same blue flame
and need for painkillers
as an athlete's bum knee
or the hay-baler's back.

And we're not yet certain
what goes bad first inside
the politician, but I suspect
it starts with the conscience
and then spreads to the heart.

But when we're finally used up,
the lucky among us die in the night
under worn sheets in our own beds,
or under the moon in those pastures
where they so kindly put us out.

The less fortunate... fall
to the bathroom floor.

MONEY CAN'T BUY YOU LIFE

~ Bob Marley, 1981

This is where the capitalists
and comedians say, *True, but...*

But what if there is no *True, but...*
on this one? What if Marley's right?

And I am not seeking easy answers
afloat on the daydreams of hippies,
but I just sat in a fancy coastal café

right next to the cigarette dangling
between insanely wealthy fingers
on an insanely wealthy left hand

while the equally wealthy right
clutched a markedly expensive
phone to a pearl-laden neck,

and the flushed brain fidgeting
between diamond-studded ears
simply could not determine

who its real friends were
yacking on the other
end of the satellite.

Everyone has got to die, but I have always believed an exception would be made in my case. Now what?

~ William Saroyan, 1981

NARCISSUS ON THE TITANIC

I too believe
this sad world
will be even sadder
without me around
to entertain it.

What a hell,
it seems,
that will be.

Though maybe
more so for me
than for others.

It's better to burn out than to fade away.

~ Kurt Cobain, 1994

DO IT RIGHT

You make a good point, Kurt.
   A rare one that we agree on.

But if your plan was to burn out
as some dark and tortured poet

grunging his way up and down
the BILLBOARD TOP 40 chart,

then maybe your last words
should've been your own,

instead of Neil Young's.

GOD HAS FORGOTTEN ME

~ Jeanne Calment, 1875 to 1997

It had to happen, eventually.

Somewhere in the population
explosion of the 21st Century,
even he was bound to lose track.

So can we blame him, that somewhere
in a small village in the south of France,
she just lived, and kept living, and kept

drinking a little port before her lunch
and dinner every day, to the point that
finally, 164 days past her 122nd birthday,

she had to go ahead and see herself out
of this worn and weary world, since he,
obviously, was not going to help her?

My God. What's happened?

~ Lady Diana, Princess of Wales, 1997

iSOLATION

A small, white,
glowing enamel apple
now bows a generation

of heads in terminal silence,
in a tumorous obedience,
to its divine applications.

We count its virtual promises
like blood-scarlet beads
on a backlit rosary.

And it consumes my daughter
in the liquid crystal flames
of its required sacrifice,

as I continue to pray
to all the old, wrong,
and analog gods.

I'M LOSING

~ Frank Sinatra, 1998

After a life of Jack Daniels,
Las Vegas lights and winning,
maybe losing is what death
would've felt like to him.

The star, once so bright,
its dying now leaves us
with a bigger darkness.

So diametric, in relief,
to a poet's Jose Cuervo
in its brown paper bag,

and all those dark nights
spent sipping and writing
on the island of his exile—

dying, more likely a means
to some kind of winning.

NO, I THINK HE'S WRITING

~ Charles Schulz, 2000
(Charlie Brown's last words
in the last Peanuts cartoon)

I hear my daughter,
    or maybe my wife,

saying this in the kitchen,
the driveway, or the garage,

a long time before they finally
find me slumped over the desk,

a flood of hardened candle wax
stuck to my elbow and the pen.

And I wonder how long it'll take
before they think to check on me.

Relax – This won't hurt.

~ Hunter S. Thompson, 2005

TO EASE THE PAIN

A sixth-grader's hand
wraps around the silver can
of cheap beer for the first time.

The young mother tries to choose
between the dark bottle of pinot noir
or the grigio, with the baby finally asleep.

The old writer slams a shot of whisky,
waits a minute, then curls a finger
around the trigger of a pistol.

Just a little something...

I am returning home, to the Earth,
to the place of my origins.

~ Bill Rodgers, 2005

TO THE EARTH

We forget
to go outside
and kneel down,
touch it... maybe

stay for while, lying
in the leaves and grass
of its immortal memory
and foreknowledge, dipping

our feet in the running waters
that carry everything—always—
down and out to the big final bath,
letting it know we are grateful

for the way it receives us
and welcomes us back,
even after so much
forgetting.

I'm going away tonight.

~ James Brown, 2006

DO, AND THEN GO

The uncomplication of death
should uncomplicate life.

All that we have done
will not be undone. But
the doing of more will be.

And if there is an afterlife,
most descriptions portray it
as a great deal of not doing.

An eternity spent with God?
What would we do? Pick a cloud?
Sit? Praise him? Without ceasing?

But if we do just... go away...
maybe I should go right ahead
and eat the all-beef kosher dog
smothered in kraut and pickles
with two or three of my wife's
smashing blue margaritas
right before we switch
the station to Magic 104.1
and make a mad dash for bed,

for to do just a little more
with our lives.

Dammit, I can't sleep.

~ Heath Ledger, 2008

TILL DEATH DO US PART

Sleep—
the co-dependent lover
I haven't found the balls
to kick out of bed and life.

True... I'd die without her.
But she loves and hates me
every damn night, the bitch.
Lures me with empty promises
of rest, maybe even sex dreams
in her deeper reaches, and then
mid-way through the night, she
decides she didn't like something
I'd said earlier, and wakes me with
the black manicured nails of her rage.

Shock takes the place of blood in veins,
and that's that, until sunrise, or before.

I've gone to a therapist. He coughs,
pulls out reading glasses, and writes
the name of a drug on a prescription.

I keep trying to explain, it's not my fault.
I am not the one with the problem. But,
I'm beginning to have my doubts now.

I'm Happy. I'm Ready.

~ Farrah Fawcett, 2009

Happy's not the word.
Ready?   Maybe?
When that time comes?

But I fight dying every day.

I don't drink a glass of water
every time I walk by it because
I like it more than añejo tequila.

I don't ease up on the Manchego
or sharp cheddar and go for more
broccoli and cauliflower instead,
because I love the way those dry
and gritty little beads in the florets
get stuck between my front teeth.

I want to live...   I'm happy here
in the hot mud of a doomed planet.

And, in spite of smug magnates,
spoiled princes and pontiffs,
I'm ready for more.

I love *you* more.

~ Michael Jackson, 2009

EYE ON THE HORIZON

When a wistful parent,
remembering a child's game,
whispers, just out of earshot,

these pitiful words to a teenager
wearing headphones and a frown,
they are... undoubtedly... true.

The Greeks had so many words
for love, but not one that could
raise the sails for this sadness.

A parent's heart for that only
teenaged daughter is much like
a retired captain's for the sea.

The ship sets out of harbor
without us now, leaving us
to our threadbare recliners

and the shipping forecast.

I'VE NOT FELT THIS WELL FOR AGES

~ Keith Floyd, 2009

Writing 159 poems about dying words
and notable epitaphs, can make a man
hungry to write about life and living.

And a reader who loves to point out
discrepancies will undoubtedly notice
there are not 159 poems in this book.

That's because poems written about
dying words and epitaphs are bound
to be pathetic, or much too sincere.

You, in particular, may have found
a few of the ones that made the cut
still a waste of your valuable hours.

To which I counter, that any book
must have a certain number of pages
for its lengthy title to fit on the spine.

All this to say: I've survived surgery
and my daughter's fifteenth year.
And things are going too well,

for now, to just sit here
and stare at any more
damned tombstones.

DON'T TRY

~ Charles Bukowski's gravestone, 1994

To spend
even a minute pondering
what he might have meant,
would be to ignore his advice.

Tricky bastard, that Bukowski.

So, forget about 'im. He's dead.

Which would also be his advice,
if ghosts were prone to giving it.

And, his epitaph does remind me
of something dad told me long ago,

right after a more than upstanding
deacon stormed out of his study
at the church in a thick cloud
of righteous indignation:

Man... that guy
is gonna overshoot heaven
as sure as hell.

Do You Have It Now?

~ John Denver, 1997

No, John. But I've been looking.
Listening. Searching for so long,
since you died before I was ready.

You know my life is your fault—
this life of songwriting, poverty, and
poems that mostly I give a damn about.

But I'm getting closer…
    closer to something…
with the lighthouse flash
of every passing year.

I can't explain it,
but I think it has to do
with what you were asking
through all the panic and static
on your plane's radio right before
it went down in Monterey Bay.

And that's vague, I know.
But I want to thank you.

    For everything…
        and for leaving me
            with the question…
                instead of the answer.

It is not our job to be loved,
it's our job to be remembered.

~ James McMurtry

Author Bio

Nathan Brown is a songwriter, photographer, and award-winning poet from Norman, Oklahoma. He served as Poet Laureate of Oklahoma for 2013/14.

He holds a PhD in English and Journalism but mostly travels now, performing readings and concerts, as well as leading workshops and speaking on the creative process and creative writing.

Nathan has published ten previous books. Most recent was the anthology *Oklahoma Poems, and Their Poets,* a finalist for the 2015 Oklahoma Book Award. And *Karma Crisis: New and Selected Poems* was a finalist for the 2013 Paterson Poetry Prize and the 2013 Oklahoma Book Award. His earlier book, *Two Tables Over,* won the 2009 Oklahoma Book Award. He has two Pushcart Prize nominations, and his CD of all-original songs, *Gypsy Moon,* came out in 2011.